THE BODY

Michael

Benedikt

THE

BODY

Wesleyan University Press
MIDDLETOWN, CONNECTICUT

Many of these poems have previously appeared elsewhere. For permission to reprint them here, and for the assignment of copyrights, grateful acknowledgment is made to the editors of the following: *Angel Hair, Ambit, Art and Literature, Choice, Lugano Review, Minnesota Review, Paris Review, Quarterly Review of Literature, The Sixties,* and *Transatlantic Review.*

"Before Going On," "An Enormous Dangling Sack-like Net," "The Eye," "Fraudulent Days," "Inside the Mystery," "Motions," "Pink Buds," "Procession," "The Saint," "Some Litanies," "Some Old Men," "A Strained Credulity," "Tears," "Time," "Thoughts," "Tulips," "The Villain," "A Visual Face," and "The Wings of the Nose" were first printed in *Poetry.*

Library of Congress Catalog Card Number: 68–27539

Manufactured in the United States of America

First edition

NOTE: *The poems are arranged in approximately chronological order*

CONTENTS

THE BODY

I

Air, air, you are the distantmost thing I know,
Not even the whales in their patterns upon and under
The sea, are more inscrutable, to me;
You carry sails of travelers to interesting places,
And adventurers, sailors, or just plain traders;
You encourage the bicyclist to mount his apparatus
And you are ever present during swimming lessons
So that when the reluctant swimmer may emerge
From the water an instant, he'll freeze;
And air, you are hanging around fetid places
Always, ready to clear the dank atmosphere
With a breath of yourself; I have found you in
The slums of the intellect even, about to puff
When the mind is hopelessly weak after travel,
And in the lines of poems, pointless to all others,
Poised like a bouquet, sprightly and colorful.

London, 1962

Tired of poultry, the experimental chemist
Slouched under the laboratory light.
His assistant, Phyllis, for whom he had
An eye, had crept out at exactly five
Leaving the mad old man there
Beneath all the fluorescent tubes.

Soon, through the window, the lunar
Rays shone. The landscape brilliantly
Lit up, by the reflections from frost.
But the old man lay among the poultry
Droppings, a victim, police had it,
Of desperate unrequited love.

Phyllis's life was changed by the event.
No sooner had she attended Georg's
Funeral, than she abandoned her old ways.
Parties all night, festivals at which
Her nudity glittered with the aspics,
Poetry readings in little cellar bars,

Her life was changed. She bought a dog.
In the park, for free, they
Fondled her near the fountain. Enough
Had soon happened to fill a lifetime.
Then, tired of the arts and sciences of men,
Phyllis crept home to gentle Peoria.

In Peoria, Phyllis was somehow unsatisfied.
Her restless ways became apparent
To her parents, and one day, as she
Was returning from the corner soda parlor

With the local plumber, her parents
Drew her aside. Our dear Phyll, they

Said, you are insufficiently happy here.
You are not the little girl we knew
Who went wincing up to the attic
Tenderly, when struck, and would not
Come down, for a week: you seem more hip
Now, and very unlikely to stay

More than an unhappy few months more here.
Why don't you get out and leave now?
Phyllis filled her bags with their money
And went down the highway, a victim
Of inherited kindliness, troubled
By remembrances of recent events.

MOTIONS

after Man Ray

Carrying in the black bundle
                        the evening paused on the road
To tug at the laces
               to peek beneath the paper
While it mumbled to itself
Then carried it another fifty feet
And stopped by the roadway
Sat down
And turned it upside down shook the package listened to it rattle
Then trotted away
Into the privacy of a little group of roadside trees
It returned smiling
                 carrying nothing
O lovely unpredictable
            hour

MR. RAINMAN

In the rain, get your hands off my trickling face!
A damp rug
                my chilled hands
Show that we have a visitor
                        A smudge
                        in a soggy grey coat
And shoes that hiss on the diningroom table
We thought he needed a shave but that shadow on Mr. Rainman's
    cheek meant he was covered with mosses and various greens
    growing there

O my pink-cheeked daughter
O my daughter in your ancient but yellowed white pinafore
                        what are you doing turning shyly

You stand out enough

The victim lay simply
On the porch
Near the window
By the shadow
Under the swing
Past the cleft
Of the house cut in two.

Not far off
Peering through the trees
You could see
The satisfied
Assassin's eye.

THE EUROPEAN SHOE

The European Shoe is constructed of grass and reed, bound up and
    wound around so that it may slip easily over the wearer's head.

In case you are an aircraft pilot, you must take care that the
    European Shoe does not creep off your foot, and begin to
    make its way carefully along the fuselage.

The European Shoe pressed against the fugitive's nose, preventing it
    from imminent departure.

The European Shoe spends summers in delightful ways. A lady feels
    its subtle and unexpected pressure the length of her decolletage.
    (It winters in pain.)

That time I lent you my European Shoe you departed with a look of
    grandeur, and in total disrepair.

The European Shoe knocks on the door of the carefree farmerette.
    "The harvest has been gathered in, ha, ha," it says, moving
    shyly forth along the edge of the couch.

I pointed to the European Shoe. I ate the European Shoe. I married
    the European Shoe.

Tears fall from the eye of the European Shoe as it waves goodbye to us
    from the back balcony of the speeding train.

It helps an old lady, extremely crippled and arthritic, move
    an enormous cornerstone. It invents a watch, which, when wound
    up tightly, flies completely to pieces.

It was a simple and dignified ceremony, distinguished for its gales
of uncontrollable laughter, in which I married the European Shoe.

If it rains, the European Shoe becomes very heavy. I failed to cross
the river, where thousands of European shoes lay capsized.

And so we lived alone, we two, the envy of our neighborhoods, the
delight of our lively hordes of children.

I saw a flightful of graceful swallows heading to distant, half-
forgotten islands over the distant seas; and in the midst of that
annually questing company, I saw the European Shoe.

It never harmed anyone, and yet it never helped anyone.

Gaily it sets out into the depths of my profoundest closet, to do battle
with the dusts of summer.

FRAUDULENT DAYS

Fraudulent days, the surfaces collapse
When against them you press your finger
The beautiful brick suit
When you scrape it is only a tinsel clothing
The whole upper stories of the building
Touched, is a seagull's back, revealed

And when I press in on you with my shynesses,
An acceleratedly decreasing circle,
Your eyes look up as if to discourage
Departure. Your eyelids constantly falling
Under the lampshade, beneath this greenish light
In this wholly improvised conviction

THE AMBITIOUS LUMP

When papa hit Geoffrey with the frying pan
It was his initial experience
And it kept on increasing and expanding
Until he was a sophisticated boy

A little stultified perhaps by his ambition
And proneness to slaughter
But we all excused him because of his penmanship
And so passed the first years of his apprenticeship.

When Geoffrey took over the presidency of the large construction
    corporation
He was at last a total cripple.
The lump had risen up day after day
And one evening had taken its ultimate revenge

Hardly recognizing the exigencies of life as men tended to live it
Geoffrey hit peak after peak.
Although detached, he had risen so high
Only the lump could elevate him any further

When I visited Buenos Aires recently
I noticed Geoffrey on top of Sugar Leaf Mountain.
He was standing there ten thousand feet above the sea level
Hitting himself over the head

MUTUAL MORTIFICATIONS

Monstrous rare irregular lives, the ones
I cannot believe
Exist, seem so funny

From where I am sitting on the lip

Of the hole in which I
Keep my daughter and mother.

In a reversed perspective
The danger of blanching would be so great!
I would have to consume only black

Day-by-day
And I do

PROCESSION

Now that I notice it is my much beloved body which has been
    drifting back and forth beneath the pier underwater
I am becoming more sympathetic to snails
After all, what do oysters want
Seals are shy
And what is the matter with putting up a playful fin among the
    swimmers

Thus we march forward into a future
Arms akimbo legs akimbo head akimbo
Hair akimbo as it gradually drifts away
There is so much that is akimbo here that there is hardly any room
    to be "awry"

Forward forward forward
Into a privileged area where a curious conglomeration
Of currents and sand has made out a little space
Out of the wind out of the rain out of the unmanageable crowds
Who flow over the sense of privacy, and among whom
Any umbrella is easily lost

Some day all things will be water that battleship
Which you see bounding on the main will be liquid or gaseous
Its captain and its crew
The spinster with her what-not shelves the teamster with his graft
The subways with their calming quality the grass with its disturbances
Lapels with all their pallor and graveyards with their sheen

All will be water all will be pouring

Descending from the skein of the firm and the packed
There is no pleasanter exercise on earth than metamorphosis
Time passes
And all the things that we love must be changed

DIVINE LOVE

A lip which had once been stolid, now moving
Gradually around the side of the head
Eye-like
The eye twisted on the end of somebody's finger and spinning
Around the sun, its ear,
And the brain aloft over the lake of the face—
Near the cataract of the body—
Like a cumulus cloud enlarged before a rainstorm:

A sound
That grows gradually in the East
Driving everything before it: cattle and rainbows and lovers
Swept on
To the table of the body at which five men and two women are
     casually sitting down to eat

THE AIDER

To be helpful
To lift up an eyelid at midnight
To observe the lack of vigor
To grasp them by one arm and drag them out of the room
                                                    and downstairs
And dress them in an old oilskin against black insects in the hall
Drag them down the front flight of stairs
And put them in the trunk of the car, locking it carefully for safety
Then to drive them out to the country
Down these deserted roads, with only the black night butterflies alert
And there, in the country, to find a quiet relaxing place
Perhaps on a knoll or in a field or under a bridge with the water
        tricklings writing maledictions on everything
And to bury them there
In the oilskin
With the insects at a little distance
(And bury them deep and undiscoverable)
—To be this helpful
Is unappreciated, often.

THE EYE

The narcissist's eye is blue, fringed with white and covered with tempting salad leaves.

The purse-stealer's eye is yellow.

The eye of the non-combatant is white. In the center is a target rendered in green and black.

The voluptuary's eye comes to a point. It is like a silo, the echo of a halo.

The gravedigger's eye is hollow. It is surrounded by a thoroughly contemporary serenity.

The dynamite salesman's eye is like a pool, in which he who leans to drink may be lost. Drifting forever, like a cloud.

The maiden's eye is tucked under.

The billiard-player's eye comes to a point. It is like a mild wine. Each billiard-player suffers from imperfect nostalgia.

The ghost's eye is green.

The poet's eye is like a candy.

The battleship captain's eye is like the light that falls in a glen, when the doe has done with drinking.

The eye of the realist is inflatable.

II

SOME LITANIES

1.

Was the arrangement made between the two couples legal?

No.

Did they spread the word around?

No.

Have you visited the two couples lately? Did you have an
interesting time? Was it illegal?

No.

What was the decoration like?

It was furnished in Swedish "modern." Strings were hanging
down in the living room. A bird flew in the window once
and out again.

Will you ever marry?

No.

Have you ever been married?

I don't remember.

Do you love your husband?

Yes.

2.

May I please have this dance?

No.

May I please have that dance?

No.

Aren't you going to wear anything to the dance?

Yes.

Are you a good dancer?

Yes.

Do you know how to dance?

No.

May I in that case have your company during the dance
    they decide to play exactly at midnight, whatever it is?
    I have fallen in love with your eyes, lips, hands
    and hair.

No.

3.

During the lapse of several years, during which I spent
    most of my time in Barcelona, was the magazine published?

Yes.

During the lapse of several years, during which I spent
    most of my time in Barcelona, was the magazine published?

No.

Aren't you absolutely sure?

No.

Aren't you absolutely sure?

Yes.

Will you ever come to Barcelona with me?

No. I am afraid to leave behind the business affairs
    of the magazine, of which I am general manager.

Are you really that conscientious?

No.

4.

Would you care to deal him the death-dealing blow?

No.

Would you care to pay him a little visit?

No.

Would you care to improve his laundry service by
making persistent inquiries?

No.

Are you really his legal guardian?

No.

Would you care to hand him this large can of
fortified beeswax?

No.

Do you have a favorite hobby?

Yes. Devoting myself entirely to that boy.

HIDING-PLACE

It is a haven climbing here under
Your hand, as it moves across the porch
Thumbing among the magazines, selecting,
As it dips into the pit of the night
And grasps the wrist of the departing.
I wish I could be one of your lovers
And could bring you food and rings
Good news and stationery,
Photographs and improved climate.
I would climb out from under your fingertips
And would leap from knee to knee.
You would surely supply me with dust particles then
For me to drop on all these beetles;
And I would roll them down mountainsides
And listen for the crushing noise.
Together we would forge a mode of life.
They would find us hidden under the sea
Just after the earth entirely collapsed,
A situation I hope will never obtain.
I like it here very much now.

TIME

The cleft in my hat
                    is bearing a little soot
A seed falls
A few fanning spears
Of grass
          are there
And now a red flower

PINK BUDS

Pink buds pink buds ah look
one of them is over there on the lawn
of your country estate
one of them is over beneath
the low and traditional linden tree another
is under that covered wagon somebody left standing out all century
pink buds pink buds my my how nice
the emblem I have been designing
intended to be symbolic of "springtime and plenty of youth"
utilizes this common motif
pink buds I see you do not peek
out of the flag of my landlord
pink buds you are the weights
which I place on the sheaves which are my thinking and musing
to hold my memory down

Pink buds I distinctly recall two
they tiptoe discreetly indian style
across the bosom of my generous one
visiting O beneficial Persephone
the country all dark summer long

TULIPS

The tulips never really hurt
As they rose up in the night
Thrashing over the bed
Thrusting themselves into various orifices in the room
Nor did the crunching
Heard in night's darkest part
Ever injure anyone innocent
However it must be understood
That when I am glad to see you
And squeeze you so much you
Might think I meant to attack you instead of greet
It definitely pains
                  especially now
                            thinking about it
                                    me

Sitting here in my remarkable apartment
Which consists of three tons
Of pressurized stuff
                Saying go

IN LOVE WITH YOU

Would you mind revealing to me exactly what is
your symbol, a tendril?
Soon my cottage will be vine-covered.
The old caretaker will find his spade and his
wheelbarrow woven together with spidery tracing,
and his fingers, arms and legs.
There will come as a matter of fact
a sobbing from all the help—what training for any lazy maids!
The smoke which has escaped the chimney
will have the shape of an arbor in which we will never sit.
And what a memo you will have established!
How much better than if you had revealed
your symbol was actually something like hogwort
or liverwurst.

THE GRAND GUIGNOLS OF LOVE

for Louis Simpson and Milton Gilman
for their suggestions on the verse

"The generosity of her love provides
Me with practically all edibles.
It is like coming constantly to table.
If only we were not in our underwear, or bare,
It would be ideal dining."

He thought he might tie his lady
Up, to a chair, to amuse them that day;
Once fixed, he would tickle mercilessly.
She arrived panting, and was soon
Attendant in her underthings
His hideous plan, upon a chair.
Then he thought: no rope there!
"Does the executioner's victim
Supply her own weapon of destruction?" she inquired.
"It would have been thoughtful,"
He replied, as yet undaunted.

"Wait," he said. "I have thought
A marvelous entertainment:
I will beat you with these chains
While you dangle from this ceiling by the foot."

She, imagining the benefit
Straightway consulted her tinted wardrobe.
The array of costumes was endless
Once they started upon them.
He never knew what she would be
And she, for her part, never knew.
Courtesan, faun and fireman they ranged

And down through mythologies and classes
They plunged, then surfaced and lay gasping.

Sitting late at table that night
Solemnly, yet not without an undertone
Of joy, they concurred
That they were lucky to have encountered.
In a world fraught with indifference and danger
Here each had come upon the rare "oral" type.
Carefully, hand in hand, they would sail away
With a sharpened sense of *savoir-faire*.

And sometimes their thoughts would travel together
To lands of such gentle events
That they would look at one another.

THE GREAT DIVAN

"Nous nous sommes souvent ennuyés, comme ici"—Baudelaire

And one of them, a sweet child, looked up
And said, though her words
Were lost in the general thrashing of that moment
"I must return soon to my parents' house
Which represents stability to me,"
Then plunged back faltering into the writhing mass

And another, whose lorgnette
Had been broken by the Dockworker from Flushing, Long Island
Genuflected beside the great divan
And abased herself by abstention
As I was later sternly told

By one of the hosts, and an old friend of mine.
"And it was curious the way they chuckled"
She said, brushing crumbs from her cuffs
"When they found themselves there
Alone, just the five of them."

SOME OLD MEN

Nobody understands the reason for these indigent sweepers being here
And coming by every evening at the edge of the Tuileries
Sweeping the garden with sweeping equipment of past days

Their eyes are dim their hands barely grip their brooms
Faggot brooms bound with old rushes and things
And they chatter with excited gestures

And should a lady go by wearing a grey fur coat
Beneath which is a frock torn partly to shreds
They begin an innocent whistling and staring at the sky

Companion of my days companion of my evenings
Oh this must be our favorite spot in the Tuileries of all
Shaded and calm and only slightly dusty

A large weight lay inside the enormous dangling sack-like net. When the breeze pressed forth, it swung in the hand; then, bit by bit, it came to a full stop.

Stooping down, we could see the outlines of the weight: they were those of a small building, a country house. It was surrounded by apple-trees in flower. Young men in rough work clothes, with rough-hewn ways, were climbing in the branches looking for apples.

The gestures they made in their search, so practical and so firm, and so inadvertently beautiful, seemed to admonish the stranger to take heart.

TEARS

The eyes that shower down upon these fields
Are obviously suspended
Their position indicates a superior elevation

                      tears
Tears

                                tears

      tears

          tears   tears

                     tears

          tears

And they run off down a ditch far into the distance

III

DANGEROUS WAYS

Creeping along upsidedown
The figure in the mirror
Remained in apparent concealment

To those of us assembled
Here underneath
Where shadows haltingly flashed past

Leaving us staring at one another
At a loss for any explanation
Where we sat. Late in the evening

Under the large lump of material and old adhesive tape in the corner
A shadow fled:
A living being

Who'd watch our errors and pathetic miscalculations
Without comment.

DEVELOPMENTS

1.
Suddenly we were overwhelmed with genuine reasons
Several of us were impressed
And one of our company threw open the window

"It was nice! It was nice!"

We had never liked it more than that previously.

2.
That night, gathered around the candlesticks
We examined it.
It raised its little head and smiled back in return

And we made it our official mascot.

3.
Now we gradually tire of our ancient playthings.
They keep coming to our attention,
Other items. Our meetings differ

How can we help investigating them?

I myself begin to feel that we must retire from our previous
    enthusiasms.

4.
This morning, the largest newspaper in the universe
Carries a headline saying

It has died during the night
Of love.

THE VILLAIN

The villain crept by on the slant
                              towards the Southwest
The brim of the hat he wore was pulled down over his eye, his nose,
    and his mouth
Against the suns
Of the days he would pass in traveling unaccompanied
Against both his suns and his sins

Low brim! it fell down to the ground
Swept over the tops of trees when the wind came
And an investigator

Trying to see into his eyes

Could see only leaves

A VISUAL FACE

Too much of your mouth slows down the reflexes to logic
And deflects the thoughts
But not enough of this particular member?

                                          I forget.

It has been so long since I have been uninvolved
In your pretty teeth and wide smile
That reminds me of the sun-goggles which summertime or wintertime
You wear.

          Three shapes, something like dashes
In dry old literature, so I celebrate you now
Not with language, my dear dumb tongue

```
                but
              H A I R
            r           h
            i  —   —  a
            a      —      i
            h                   r
```

COIFFURE

Hair! it was hair
That increased the enthusiasm

Of all those standing around
Waiting for some love

Any love—but really only
Hair made them care—

Hair piled up into prodigious mountaintops and considerable ranges,
Hair in groves, hair in lofts

Hair that you could balance
On the knee, like an act

In vaudeville. So come sit
On my lap now, hair,

It doesn't matter whose hair
Or what hair, goat hair

Or monkey hair, but wear hair
Of some kind

When you come to me, to me alone, all shaded
By hats.

A ROOM

The furniture intertwined with flowers
The doorways ambiguous
The lintels desperate

I have been living in this large midtown hotel for years; when I'm
   bored I stick my head out of the window and observe the
   transactions of perverts. Yes! they are more generous than they
   are ever credited with being; but Oh! they have no love!

Not only that, but my sky
Is one huge bloom every Friday

There is a girl who comes in the door.
Her face is crushed petals and her teeth are vines,
Her eyes are grey as a tree-trunk,
And when she departs, she leaves
Traces of earth and moss on the carpet

Having a room *here* is becoming increasingly like the rental
Of a schooner.

GEMINI EMBLEM

I was so undecided
I seemed constantly to be leaping to my feet and then
    sitting down in one incredibly powerful motion

People stopped in front of my location
To observe the phenomena

Besides that, I couldn't sleep,
Bit my nails, felt dizzy after dancing,
And I had this picture in my mind of carrying around my lungs
    as if they were valises I was trying to smuggle through
    customs, perhaps as if to slip my heart through
    my mind

There I was, at thirty,
A blur on the horizon.

A BELOVED HEAD

A beloved head, truly, but the mouth part was operated
By a small treadle
Located just outside near the corner of the lawn;
The ears by a lightswitch
And the eyes by two faucets, mounted inside the writingdesk.
The hair was operated by a kind of abacus
On which one tried not to lose count of possible developments there;
When it hung down loose it could envelop the attention of the operator.

The body of the beloved was operated from an enormous panel
Covered with hundreds of dials
One had to climb up to it by means of a ladder
Daring that only after a refresher-course from the handbook which
        came with either the previous instrument, or the previous beloved,
        the operator can never remember which
How often that body would suddenly whirl around
With a gesture so gentle and rare
One could not seriously comprehend that one had created it

—Nor even the way it arched its back and stretched
        in the commonest of yawns; or adjusted jewelry
        come slightly awry (one had accidentally brushed
        against a small throttle located near the knee)—

And sometimes the controlling mind collapses.
Just look at the way the operator is slumped over now.
He is tired, his head hurts, his hand is exhausted
In fact he has fallen asleep there in his chair.
And the beloved, head and body, is passing the time until the next
        awakening

By sitting around and sewing, presently the sleeve
Of a doll's kimono which she has decided to give to a Japanese friend of
    hers who collects such things

THE SPIRIT

Touches of the things upon which we press
Clutch back now; we reach out in thought
And feel their hands in ours
And together we walk down the long road between the summerlit trees
In the park, watching out for the rapists. We do not see any more
In our room full of glossy furnitures
But feel them (the way we feel the sagging willowyness of that tree
Becoming emblematic of our tenuousness).
They are rising in their lumps and patterns
And we identify them with the various understructurings
Of the body we are forced to use
Whenever we set forth to explore the atmosphere of the universe, by
    breathing.

They have all become the actual people,
We the things.

SOME FEELINGS

The feelings go up into the air
Rising in lines that are straight until they bump
Into something
A building
With its roof overhanging, a judge
Who is looking out of the window attempting to see that nurse
Changing uniforms which are transparent anyway in a neighboring
    indoor hospital yard
Music (the feelings sift through little drifting notes from a radio);
Then they continue
Rising so swiftly and so purely they seem to supersede all objects

Only somebody
At the level of the ground may see
That each feeling is connected by a thread to a forehead, an arm, or
    a leg
And that individuals
At the heights of their tragic moments
Resemble porcupines or pincushions.

ADVANCING

Simply to think about some things
Is to accomplish them; you turn your head
And the earth vanishes
And what you see is a permeated heaven

Of stars and lattices and everything flourishing
And you have accomplished it all
Almost by accident, as if while lifting

Enormous weights from cloud plateau to cloud plateau
Your thought had somehow turned to something solid
And at last you felt the wholesome atmosphere

Of doubt

A STRAINED CREDULITY

1.

A strained credulity:
It sags
Suspended there in air
With nobody even placing a stick under it
(The way a toothpick might be placed beneath the eye of a
      bon vivant to help him keep a sharper watch
      all during the many activities of the day)
Or adjusting it
So that at least the weight of disbelief
Might be distributed more evenly among the four corners.

2.

Oh how much fun are you having tonight
Man in the top hat, white silk scarf, yellow matte spats, heavy
      lead cane, with the sink stoppers stuck in your ears against
      the sound of your own incredible gaiety?

EVENTS BY MOONLIGHT

Some intense event dictated a poem;
Poem and event had come closer together than ever before.
It was as if, in passing,
The event had pressed its own image against the page
And its very shape had left a mark

The hand lay useless on top of the desk. It smoked.

The pencil fell under the desk unsharpened and broken
And the moon rising over the very intimate room
Pressed itself very hard against the window where the groups of
    lovers had recently been assembled.

A whole landscape of future events was illuminated out there
        in the room
But none could be without the moon's being:
The dust of events was never shed on the paper except under
    the moonlight

JOY

How can I get through that innocence?
Jump through, and land in a damp swamp?
No, I'd rather go bicycling

Around, and enjoy its transparent squalor
Starred with flowers so magnificent
Only the most rotted self-deception could impel them.

Another thing I like doing a lot
Is helping you across busy boulevards
With a specially enlargeable hand

Implying friendly aid at first,
Secondly, a growing degree of passion;
Then I inflate it and make it throb! I also enjoy

Watching you tremble in deserted underground tunnels,
Your wonderful trembling too when we are side by side at midnight,
And kayaking in mid-Atlantic, alone.

FOR LOVE OR MONEY: TWO COMPLAINTS

(1)

Even to those of us who remained sensible of the various attributes of
    "X" there were certain aspects of her talent and judgment about
    which we felt that we were beginning to become dubious
Her art, for example,
It made you feel like removing your eyes
And the topmost portion of your head so as to facilitate the performance
    of a lobotomy, enabling all the various loose extra-visual
    implications of her work to be dropped, thus abolishing overtones
Her sentences
Which shot forth all over the apron of the fan-like fluted expanses
    which in imagination we saw, spreading out of her head, ruined
    and stained
Her lovers
Who moved around at night utterly shapeless and strange, so that
    others glimpsing them, and after conversation, would remark:
    "Agh! phooey! you wouldn't catch us talking to them at even the
    dullest cocktail party ever thrown!"
(Which takes care of her abilities as hostess, for she was the thrower
    of the party to which the speaker just referred)
Her husband
Who blew smoke all over her whenever he could, it is true; and yet to
    whom, certainly, no lover was superior
Her sense of values
Her children
Her ability to take the proper precautions when necessary
And her ability to choose really only the very *best* photographs from
    among the large mass assembled casually for eventual selection for
    placement in her family photograph album

All this! And yet how come I could remain sensible of her attributes?
   Her swiftness of speech and her purity of diction! Treasuring
   up the very memories
I thought I had canceled and concealed, in some kind of a big bag
   which I dropped into darkness every night, but which I was
   certainly inefficient at disposing of, for look now how it darkens
   my door again today—as her voice my ears, my eyes her hair—
And I am gradually beginning to grow dubious about my own talent
   for living.

(2)

Have a little money and your goods
Come and go quite properly—
Canned and boxed and bundled
Pass so there is hardly any opportunity
To be measuredly spending.
Try getting down to your last cent!
Then with discountenancing suddenness
Even your spare toilet paper supply
Seems acceleratedly dwindled.

AT NIGHT

The things left undone
Are looking at us with their enquiring glances

They see through our schedule
They know we have been putting them off a lot

That somewhere
The things done
Are sitting around, listening to my record-player, smoking my cigars,
  wearing my slippers, and drinking wine from my long-stemmed
  glasses, and feeling very well in general
Because they are the things attended to initially.

It's arbitrary, though: I would just as soon have kissed you behind the
  thigh where your hair starts to become unexpectedly curly
As on that particular spot beneath your ear which curves like a rowboat
Overturned and found
On a steep beach
At night.

THE OBSERVATION TOWER

Watching a departure: pressed up against your visage
To investigate
I noticed

Nothing
Except a caravan, setting forth with its camels, packets, drivers,
     whips and tents
And in the lines around your mouth

Somebody was tilling the soil of some distant locale,
Hoeing. Yes,
The telescope view was indeed blocked

By the face of the individual
Against
Which it was pressed.

THE SWIMMER'S TEARS

An underwater sob. The swimmer's tears
Resulted in bubbles
Which, emerging, gave rise to the thought:

                                  just as here
In the water, which is the usual medium of tears
A sob bubbles
So, in the atmosphere which you produce

                               by locating your head in it
Everything's reversed:
Around you it's nicer not to be too nice

                               and not kissing you at all
Is never to get out of bed even once.
So the swimmer, his shiny full length once emerged,
Was seen, atop his glistening watersogged casque

                               of hair
To have a frog.
Now I see: from the beginning, Love, this creek was never
Reasonably navigable.

BEFORE GOING ON

An entire curvature, for a change,
There are so many which are broken up into arcs,
So much criss-crossing
And going up and down
With this breathing,
With the construction
Of this body.
This curvature
Is the one which proceeds
Down below the shoulderblade
And which is terminated suddenly
By a really unbelieveable sweep. Look—it tries to scoop up the eyes!
Oh!—my eye just has to rest a little while, please,
On that little stable plateau in the hollow
Just at the back of this lady's waist
Before going on.

AFTER HIS THIRTY–FIRST BIRTHDAY PARTY

My tired smile
        It lies down on the job
                (On the labor of laughter, I mean)
It lies down on the settee
           See
            the smile just lying there
In my livingroom
Propped up like a crescent moon

INSIDE THE MYSTERY

Inside the mystery
Gone into a crouch
In hopes of fitting somehow, so as to have some kind of an opportunity
To remain, where it is warm
And shapeless, and pleasant to crouch and lurch.
The light in here is somewhat pink.
But it illuminates next to nothing.
(It is as if a lady
Had pulled on a glove over her hand, and you;
And you were half expecting
It to come peeling back
Again, and back
Off the shoulder and under the chin
And as far back as over the hill and to grandmother's house.)
Inside the mystery
It was better than having a light
Just to grope around
With careful claws and paws
Caressing to determine anything you could ever learn,
Writing only poetry,
Making only love.

MILLWHEEL

The motion is going on
That driving, by which the wind
Is forced
Upward, lifting the edge of the hair, or,
If a wig, that wig
Which ascends afar, finally to land somewhere in a tree;
And yet that very motion may change
And leave objects
Resting, and in such a state of repose
That, chipping away at even casual daily events with a hammer
May accomplish little. They are so set. A few shards,
The relics,
Remain, of what one had meant to be the most considerable
    investigations
Of the self. The self? It is unquestionably an experiment
Defined in the shifting
Of things, as they move forth and back:
Eyes which once had the color
Of a sea one had remembered and liked
A sort of blue
But which, studied beneath some isolated internal lens,
Turned a personal
Grey.

THE WAY THINGS SETTLE

There will always be a distance
Even when things are pressing
Against one another, so hard

That crockery expresses a fluidity.
There will always be a gap to see through

And when the clouds seem to separate
So far, that the sky is
Almost embarrassingly present

There won't be any place to lie down.
But your complexion will seem transparent.

In all the various directions
Things are forming a configuration
That will be hard to break.

IV

THOUGHTS

Excuse me, isn't that you I see concealed underneath there
Inside the shield, or conning tower, of your head,
Your eyes looking out of the perforations in your flesh?
How can you think you can see from out of liquid, anyway? Are
    rain puddles watching me even now,
And can ducts which punctuate the underground of a field
Examine it at will for buried treasure? Is the rain outside your
    window a voyeur, then? Deep down under all that, though,
Underneath the liquids and the various unobservant stuffs
There is a spirit, shifting around from foot to foot.

THE SAINT

It seemed cruel to him that he should have stepped on the insect while
    it was upsidedown trying to give birth
Wrong, that the mark it left was so large on the underside of his shoe
It always seemed to him that it was a mistake to lapse into casual
    habits
That, in truth, the only pattern that should be followed without
    evoking the maximum of deliberateness and consciousness
Was the pattern of being crushed up oneself

All other events it seemed to him should have approximately the same
    off-handedness as the digging of someone toward the light in a
    collapsed mine-shaft
And so he took on the lineaments of effort:

The clothing covered with traces of fine powder from head to foot
The shoes letting light leak in
The string tie burnished by the blazing black sun of miraculous amounts
    of carbon
The headgear peppered by coke
And behold! the earmuffs and eyeglasses as light as butterfly wings,
    but beating back the current of some vast catastrophe, life.
Only the parts of the body that showed—the face and wrists—were a
    little older now.

AFTER A READING OF McLUHAN, WHOM I ADMIRED

Will you complain about old-fashioned furniture?
Forever, a mode of knowing
Will be retained on the inside of the human head
But the furniture will gradually embarrass you
And tomorrow you may throw it away

If only it were possible for a person to recline on a planet
Using the north polar cap as an ottoman
The south polar cap as a pouf
And the equator as a kitchen. It would crowd the house;
Yet the brain is never quite occupied.

The changes going on around outside the building here
Leave the brain the same blue lump it always was;
You may try to adjust but always truly contemporary events
Will be judged with thoughts a little older than they are;
Throw away your head

THE WINGS OF THE NOSE

The wings of the nose
I sense them fluttering
Making a passenger
Out of the whole olfactory system
And the brain flies along just for fun
Where are you going O wildest of widely wandering wings
Where are you taking us, my Sweetie and me?

"I am taking you someplace where you will like it
I am trying to find a place where you can rest
    and enjoy the most important sense of things of all, which is mine.
Haven't you given up other pleasures yet?
    Touch, which is just an irritation
    Taste, which I view with distaste
    Hearing, which is designed simply to put a strain on you
    Sight, which is something I have never quite been able to see
Just in case you haven't
                come with me now
          aloft in my sensational flying machine
Spend all your time
Wandering with me all day long, not to the places you want to go,
    but to places you can't resist going
Let your schedule of appointments be organized by waftings
    O follow follow

So you will say
At the end of the day
The odor of decay
Is the best and the strongest and the sweetest:
The smell of fire on bone
Of rich earth"

THE BATHROOM MIRROR

Nothing is going to get elucidated any more around here, we rely
On the natural course of events to explain itself;
And the way we are leaning forward, shading our ears and cupping our
    eyes
And the blank looks on our faces
Tell us not what we need to know, but only
Who it is that is looking and listening

The bathroom mirror is revealed as the site of revelation
At 11:35 P.M., on the last Friday of October, 1967, its truth is told
The truth of the bathroom mirror with its toothbrushholder, its
    fingermarked waterglasses, the twisted toothpaste tube, the
    false eyelashes and the razor
Revelation revelation
Revelation of the thing we have always been closest to.
Now, without our having to ask it to, it shows us all the depth of
    the things we have known and loved the best

THE DEBRIS OF THE BODY

The debris of the body is piled up all around the foot of the statue
And is scattered around the landscape.
It starts on the statue's shoe
And then thins out until it comes to a river, where light debris
　　drifts, and the heavy debris sinks, hitting a fish on the head.
The small town is nestled in a peaceful valley, the debris of the
　　body comes and covers it; now it nestles under ten feet of
　　garbage
A photographer was photographing a lovely mountaintop locale for a
　　liquor-store calendar until the debris of the body came and
　　smudged the lens, blurring the photo, inundating the photographer
A grizzly bear climbs a tree to escape its flows
Like a decade's lemmings—if they were slower—or the sea itself,
　　it creeps to the sea. The light debris drifting, the heavy
　　hitting some other fish on the head.
There, the sea is inundated with the flower of fallen hair, worn skin,
　　fingernail parings, nose pickings, oozed blood, used sperm
　　(love's leavings!), annoying old scabs, tears accidentally
　　escaped in wind, tears meant to be wept, the nether wastes,
　　the shit and piss of the skin, superannuated wart parts, etc.

PYROMANIAC'S LAMENT IN SPRING

"I see, I see
In spite of all my hard work, *them*
Returned and resumed.
Like a flame coming across burning floorboards, stepped on repeatedly,
    harder and harder, faster and faster
They are a danger;
As much a danger as if flowers began to flourish from roadside lumps of
    debris

"Already I see a pair of busy hands taking up stitching and knitting
    needles, thrown down into their wicker bowl as the curtains caught;
The ladder with blackened top step and broken rungs below is removed
    from the second-story windowsill and placed back in the garage;
Pieces of broken glass, lying like jewels on the lawn, leap back up to
    form a bathroom window;
Shoes left behind as the inhabitants tried to flee want to be refitted
    to feet;
The switched-off old stove that exploded anyway is turned on again, the
    odors of the strange vegetables and fleshes of that black house
    begin to permeate the street, back, black;
Slyly returned to the bedroom wall is the poster you could see from the
    street of the nude, all belly, white and gleaming;
Blades of grass begin to prickle the ground near the basement window
    from which, years ago, good horizontals of cleansing flame once
    emerged;
Fine hair is restored;
A Saint Bernard big enough to ride, trapped once behind a locked
    screen door, walks the floor again. Its back and shoulders
    are tingling
And from the heaps of knitting still to be completed emerges a
    single baby's bootie in bright red."

OLD SCHOOL TIES

It's difficult in this maze of footsteps of friends superannuated
    to keep track.
It somewhat resembles the attempt to constantly calculate where every
    mouse may be in a deserted cheese-works behind the city dump,
    so as to be able to reply sharply at any given instant, in case an
    inspector comes by with his cap and his clip-board at the ready
Or maybe it's more like juggling with trick clubs that fall apart with
    every other throw. But I hear them constantly tiptoeing backward
Inside the remains of the lives we occupied when we knew one another
    better
But never coming out into the new life, which is interesting because it
    is difficult not to become dead in sooner.

When will it be possible again to share the richness of how little we
    had experienced?
How soon will the new life begin?

THE GUARDIAN ANGEL

The guardian angel spreads out his wings and they stretch from
    the department store on the corner to the Riverside Park gazebo
His feet are in the middle of 98th Street at the center of the sidewalk
    in front of my building
He has been there since I came here, examining me for extravagances,
    inspecting, and dictating the proper phrases to use in Poetry
He arranged for my last writing assignment, the one that paid reasonably
    well, the intellectual job, the one for the *Chinese Opera Flower*
    Gazette.
Someday, when I am one hundred, I know he will arrange suitable
    employment as poet-in-residence atop the Empire State Building
    or else establish my chair as Gardener at Bennington.
There he is, hunched up in silhouette against the streetlight.
As I pass by this cold morning at 6 A.M., twirling my top hat on my
    reveler's cane, I try to shake his wing to say hello finally for the
    first time, and ask him in out of the snow that is obviously going
    to fall

New York, 1967

Distinguished contemporary poetry in cloth and paperback editions

ALAN ANSEN: *Disorderly Houses* (1961)

JOHN ASHBERY: *The Tennis Court Oath* (1962)

ROBERT BAGG: *Madonna of the Cello* (1961)

MICHAEL BENEDIKT: *The Body* (1968)

ROBERT BLY: *Silence in the Snowy Fields* (1962)

TURNER CASSITY: *Watchboy, What of the Night?* (1966)

TRAM COMBS: *saint thomas. poems.* (1965)

DONALD DAVIE: *Events and Wisdoms* (1965); *New and Selected Poems* (1961)

JAMES DICKEY: *Buckdancer's Choice* (1965) [National Book Award in Poetry, 1966]; *Drowning With Others* (1962); *Helmets* (1964)

DAVID FERRY: *On the Way to the Island* (1960)

ROBERT FRANCIS: *The Orb Weaver* (1960)

JOHN HAINES: *Winter News* (1966)

EDWIN HONIG: *Spring Journal: Poems* (1968)

RICHARD HOWARD: *The Damages* (1967); *Quantities* (1962)

BARBARA HOWES: *Light and Dark* (1959)

DAVID IGNATOW: *Figures of the Human* (1964); *Rescue the Dead* (1968); *Say Pardon* (1961)

DONALD JUSTICE: *Night Light* (1967); *The Summer Anniversaries* (1960) [A Lamont Poetry Selection]

CHESTER KALLMAN: *Absent and Present* (1963)

PHILIP LEVINE: *Not This Pig* (1968)

LOU LIPSITZ: *Cold Water* (1967)

JOSEPHINE MILES: *Kinds of Affection* (1967)

VASSAR MILLER: *My Bones Being Wiser* (1963); *Onions and Roses* (1968); *Wage War on Silence* (1960)

W. R. MOSES: *Identities* (1965)

DONALD PETERSEN: *The Spectral Boy* (1964)

MARGE PIERCY: *Breaking Camp* (1968)

HYAM PLUTZIK: *Apples from Shinar* (1959)

VERN RUTSALA: *The Window* (1964)

HARVEY SHAPIRO: *Battle Report* (1966)

JON SILKIN: *Poems New and Selected* (1966)

LOUIS SIMPSON: *At the End of the Open Road* (1963) [Pulitzer Prize in Poetry, 1964]; *A Dream of Governors* (1959)

JAMES WRIGHT: *The Branch Will Not Break* (1963); *Saint Judas* (1959); *Shall We Gather at the River* (1968)